This edition published 2004 by
Mercury Books
20 Bloomsbury Street
London WC1B 3JH
ISBN 1-904668-71-2

Publisher: Felicia Law
Design director: Tracy Carrington
Project manager: Karen Foster
Author: Gerry Bailey
Editor: Rosalind Beckman
Designed by: Jacqueline Palmer
assisted by Fanny Level, Will Webster
Cartoon illustrations: Steve Boulter (Advocate)
and Andrew Keylock (Specs Art Agency)
Make-and-do: Jan Smith
Model-maker: Tim Draper
further models: Robert Harvey, Abby Dean
Photo studio: Steve Lumb
Photo research: Diana Morris
Scanning: Acumen Colour
Digital workflow: Edward MacDermott

Printed by D 2 Print Singapore

Photo Credits
AKG Images: 5t, 9 inset, 13t, 21t, 25t, 28t, 37t, 41t.
Bob Battersby/Eye Ubiquitous: 14b.
John Dakers/Eye Ubiquitous: 26b. James DavisTravel Photography: 29b.
Michael Edrington/The Image Works/Topham: 10b. Mary Evans PL: 33t.
B Gibbs/Trip: 22b. A Lambert/Trip: 38b. NASA: 18b.
Photogenes: 34b. Photri/Topham: 6b. Topham: 9t, 42b.

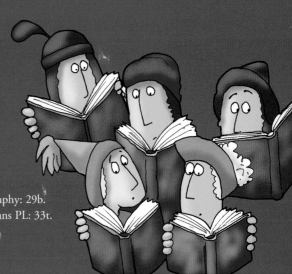

Crafty
Inventions

AGE OF NEW IDEAS

Contents

Mercury Junior
20 BLOOMSBURY STREET
LONDON WC1B 3JH

How can I capture the town?

Sir Raymond stands on a small hill and looks at the enemy town. He wants to throw heavy rocks at the bowmen who guard the town walls in order to rescue Lady Garterbilt. But he can't get close because the bowmen are very skilled. He needs a really powerful hurling machine.

If Sir Raymond can get into the town, he can rescue Lady Garterbilt. But while enemy bowmen fire from the low hill above the town, he will be sending many of his men to certain death. And even the fair Lady Garterbilt is not worth the risk.

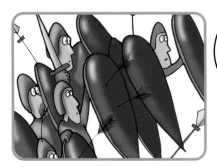

Sir Raymond's men can get closer to the bowmen by holding their shields up for protection. But that isn't close enough. And they have no bows of their own, just swords and spears. Sir Raymond needs to throw something heavy at them.

I need a powerful weapon that can hurl boulders at the town from a safe distance.

WHAT CAN HE DO?

- He could march his army close to the bowmen, then get his men to jump up and down shouting insults. It might scare the enemy - but then it might not!

- He could get his biggest soldiers to wear armour and throw stones at the enemy bowmen. But he might as well throw the soldiers.

- What if he asked his carpenters to build a huge bow catapult to shoot spears? That might do some damage.

- Instead of spears, he could shoot small boulders from the large catapults. They'd do even more damage, but they'd need more power.

I must think on a larger scale. I'll build a huge catapult. But instead of bow power, I'll use the power of a rope twisted around a pole. When it's released, it will unwind with great force, sending the catapult arm flying forward.

A trebuchet's missile was placed in a sling, which was then released by a catch.

A trebuchet

A **trebuchet**, a type of catapult, was a powerful medieval war machine used to hurl huge rocks at an enemy fortress. It was developed from the Greek and Roman catapults. Catapults, such as the trebuchet, are based on the **lever**, but others also use a twisting force called **torque** to give them power. A trebuchet could shoot heavy boulders up to 135kg in weight half a kilometre away.

Trebuchets were developed during the 13th century, and were especially effective against castles. They could sling large stones over the castle walls or at the archers who stood on top of them. Fired at a speed of over 160kph, a **missile** from a trebuchet could break through the thick walls of a castle or fortified town, making it an important siege weapon.

Torque

Torque is the amount of effort that is needed to twist a shaft or pole. It can be described more simply as twisting power. Cars use the torque, or twisting power, of their engine to turn the wheels. The faster a car goes, the less torque it needs.

Torque is used whenever a machine needs twisting power to make it work. This is especially true of heavy machines. A train, for instance, requires huge torque to get its bulk moving out of a station. Some catapults also use twisting energy for power. A rope is twisted around a pole that is fixed to the base of the lever, or arm, of the catapult. Then the pole is turned to twist the rope tightly and lower the arm.

This plane is being catapulted into the air from an aircraft carrier.

ANIMAL MISSILES

A catapult was usually located with huge boulders. But when a town or castle was under siege, soldiers might lob dead cows or horses over the walls in the hope of poisoning wells or infecting the inhabitants with disease!

Inventor's words

catapult
lever
missile
torque
trebuchet

Make your own catapult

You will need

- plank of wood
- nails • hammer
- wooden block
- clothes peg
- rubber bands • card
- polystyrene blocks
- cardboard tube • wire
- long stick
- plastic bottle
- cane • string
- paper cups • glue

1 With help from an adult, hammer a nail into one end of the plank and bend it over. Nail a wooden block to the other end and attach a peg by twisting a rubber band around it.

2 Wrap card around 3 polystyrene blocks to make a tower. Cover the top with half a cardboard tube to form a roof. Fix a wire hoop to the roof to hold the firing arm.

3 Take the long stick and loop a thick rubber band to one end. Fix the bottom of a plastic bottle to the other end to make the launch cup. Tie a piece of cane to the cup end of the firing arm with string.

4 Glue 3 paper cups to house your ammuntion to the board. Now slide the arm into place as shown.

5 To use your catapult, load the cup and press the peg to fire!

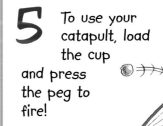

Experiment with different kinds of ammunition

How can I jump safely?

Leonardo has designed a flying machine and wants to find a way to drop things out of the machine without damaging them. Ideally, he would like the pilot to be able to jump and fall through the air slowly to land without hurting himself. How can he slow down a pilot's fall?

Leonardo often climbs up his ladder and drops old clay pots of different sizes and shapes to the ground below. He wants to see if their size or weight affects the way they fall. But even the smallest pots plunge to the ground quickly and break. Somehow, he needs to slow them down.

How can I slow down my plummeting pots – and my poor pilots?

He knows that light objects such as feathers and paper fall to the ground more slowly than heavier ones. If he finds out why, he will be able to slow things down as they fall through the air.

WHAT CAN HE DO?

- Maybe he could fix wings to the pots. The wings might slow a pot down, but they could cause it to float away altogether!

- He knows it's important to catch a lot of air. He also knows that sails catch the wind well. But a sail might not be strong enough to hold a heavy pot - or a pilot for that matter!

- What if he attached a small tent to the top of a pot, which would hang underneath? The tent would catch the air and slow the pot down - but it wouldn't be very stable.

I know, I'll make a square frame and attach four triangles of material to it that meet at the top - just like a tent or pointed roof. Then I'll use four cords to attach it to the pot. That way, my tent roof will catch lots of air.

Although Leonardo da Vinci designed a parachute, it's not known if he ever made one.

Slow descent

A **parachute** is used to lower people or objects slowly through the air and allow them to land safely. The part of the parachute that catches the air is called an **envelope** or **canopy**, and is usually rectangular or shaped like an umbrella. Parachutes are made from lightweight fabrics. The first parachutes were made from silk, but since the 1940s nylon has been used.

Cords called **suspension lines** lead from the envelope to a harness that holds the person or object. When the parachute is closed, it folds into a small pack. A **ripcord** is used to open the pack and release the parachute. Parachutes were first used to descend from gas-filled balloons in the late 18th century. Now they are used for jumping out of planes, landing soldiers and sky-diving.

Air resistance

When air resists, or tries to slow down, an object travelling through it, this is called **air resistance**. This resistance happens because moving things rub up against the gases that make up the air. A piece of paper drifts gently to the ground because air resistance acts on its surface and slows it down. If you drop a marble, it does not feel much air resistance because of its round, smooth shape.

The first planes were slowed down by air resistance. The landing gear and other parts of the plane rubbed against the air. Engineers speeded up the planes by making landing wheels that could be pulled up, and by **streamlining** the shape of the plane.

Air resistance can also be an advantage – it slows down a parachute so that people falling through the air can drift slowly and safely to the ground.

SHOOTING STARS

Air resistance can create heat. The faster something travels through the atmosphere, the hotter it becomes. Meteorites hurtle through the atmosphere at great speed, finding huge air resistance. They become so hot they glow and look like fast-moving stars.

Modern parachutes use air resistance to glide through the air.

Inventor's words

air resistance
canopy
envelope
parachute
ripcord
streamline
suspension lines

Make a paper parachute

You will need

- coloured tissue paper
- glue • string
- sticky tape
- cardboard
- pencil • paints
- brush • scissors

1 Cut out 2 large squares of tissue paper. Glue the layers together and then trim.

2 Attach equal lengths of string to each corner of the parachute with some tape.

4 Tie your parachutist to the four lengths of string.

3 Draw a parachutist on a piece of cardboard. Cut out and paint.

5 Take your parachute outside and let the wind carry it away.

How can I see more clearly?

Guido wants to become a scribe. The letters on the pages of the manuscript he needs to copy are quite large. Even so, Guido can't read them easily any more. Yet he is determined find a way to get a job in the manuscript room.

Guido's eyes have worsened over the years. When he was younger, he was able to read even small words easily. Now, though, he wants to work in the monastery, writing manuscripts. But he can't see things up close very well. Everything seems to be blurred.

He tries holding the manuscripts at arms' length. But that doesn't help. Then, in a dusty corner, he spies a small piece of glass that dips in the middle. Idly, he picks it up and looks through it – all of a sudden, everything seems clearer!

All this reading is ruining my eyesight. What shall I do?

WHAT CAN HE DO ?

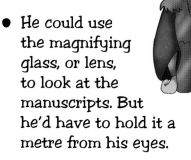

- He could use the magnifying glass, or lens, to look at the manuscripts. But he'd have to hold it a metre from his eyes.

- Maybe a glassmaker could make big sheets of glass to cover the pages of each manuscript.

- The dip, or hollow, in the glass, or lens, seems to be the key to seeing clearly. But looking for the right lens could take days, or even weeks.

- Anyway, Guido's eyes aren't the same. Each needs a different lens. He also needs something to hold two lenses. But what?

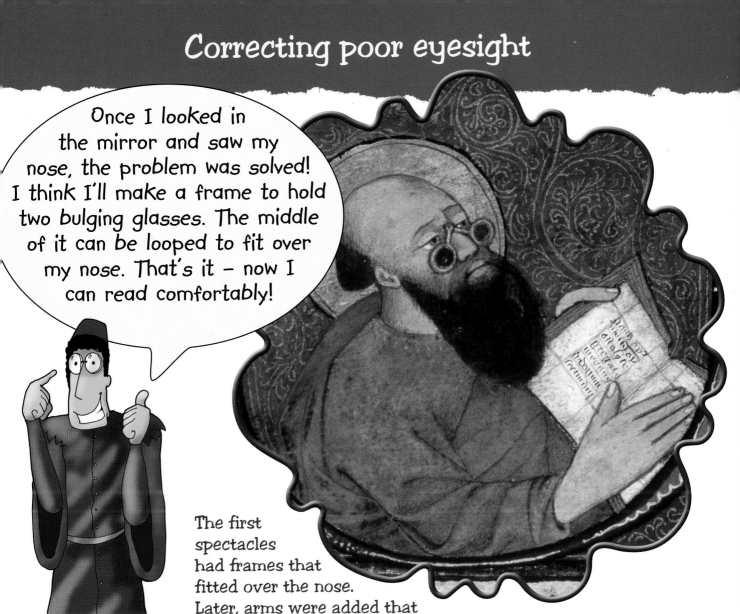

Once I looked in the mirror and saw my nose, the problem was solved! I think I'll make a frame to hold two bulging glasses. The middle of it can be looped to fit over my nose. That's it – now I can read comfortably!

The first spectacles had frames that fitted over the nose. Later, arms were added that fitted over the ears.

Easy to see

Spectacles, or glasses, are frames that contain **lenses**. They help people who have poor eyesight to see clearly. The first spectacles were probably made in Italy around 1280, but they may have been used in China before that. Generally, spectacles are fitted with **convex** or **concave** lenses. Convex lenses bulge outwards; they help people who are long-sighted, or who have difficulty seeing things close up. Concave lenses bend inwards to make a hollow; they help people who are short-sighted, or cannot see things far away. Today, most people wear spectacles with plastic rather than glass lenses, as plastic is lighter than glass and less likely to break. Contact lenses, small pieces of plastic worn directly on the eye, were developed during the 1950s.

Refraction

Refraction describes the change of direction that happens when light passes from one substance to another. When a ray of light enters or leaves a transparent, or see-through, object such as a lens, it is refracted, or changes direction. The lenses of a telescope, for instance, refract light from the stars.

Opticians use refraction when they make spectacles. A concave lens, one that curves inwards, refracts light outwards. This changes the way a person sees an object through his glasses. When light hits a normal eye, the rays focus on a part of the eye called the **retina**. When the eye is short-sighted, the rays focus in front of it. Concave lenses change the direction of the rays so they focus properly on the retina. Convex lenses refract light inward to correct long sight.

DOUBLE VISION

Some people need help seeing both up close and far away. In the 1700s, an American inventor, scientist and statesman called Benjamin Franklin solved the problem. He invented bifocals.

These are spectacles with two lenses combined into one. The lower part helps people to read; the upper part helps them see more distant objects.

An optician tests eyes to see what kind of lens will be needed.

Inventor's words

bifocal
concave
convex • lens
optician
refraction
retina
spectacles

Make spectacular specs

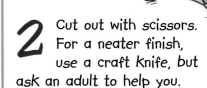

You will need

- coloured card • pencil
- scissors
  or craft knife
- clear acetate
- glitter glue
- sequins

1 Draw some wacky-shaped spectacle frames on to pieces of coloured card.

2 Cut out with scissors. For a neater finish, use a craft knife, but ask an adult to help you.

3 Cut pieces of clear acetate to size and glue to the back of the frames.

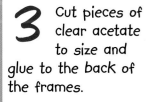

4 Fold the arms back and decorate with glitter and sequins.

5 Put on your funky designer specs and dazzle your friends!

How can I get rid of waste?

Cities are growing bigger, dirtier and less healthy as more people come to live there. Joseph is forced to duck whenever someone empties their chamber pot out of an upstairs window. Something has to be done!

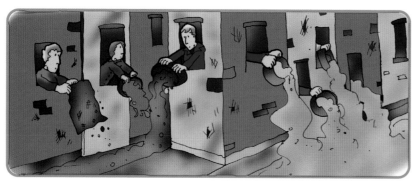

It isn't just in the streets that things are bad. Few houses have good sanitation. Outside toilets, called water closets, sometimes empty straight into a ditch, canal or even rivers. Rivers such as the Thames in London are becoming more and more polluted. And this causes disease.

> There must be a way of disposing of waste without holding my nose!

Joseph wants to find a way of getting rid of household waste quickly, and in a way that will still make the house a pleasant place to live in.

WHAT CAN HE DO?

- He could tell everyone who visited to cross their legs until they left the house.

- He could move to a house that had a river running underneath it. But that might be hard to find. And, anyway, the river would become dirty and smelly.

- What if he hired someone to stand with a bucket of water outside the toilet? But who would want the job?

- Maybe he could rig up a bucket of water with a rope attached high over the toilet bowl. The rope could be pulled each time and the bucket refilled. But some kind of storage tank would work better.

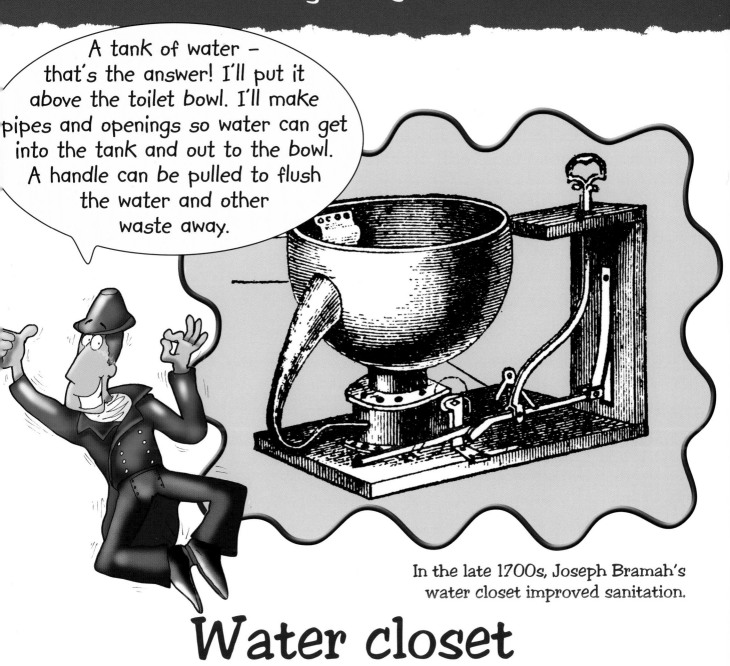

A tank of water – that's the answer! I'll put it above the toilet bowl. I'll make pipes and openings so water can get into the tank and out to the bowl. A handle can be pulled to flush the water and other waste away.

In the late 1700s, Joseph Bramah's water closet improved sanitation.

Water closet

Water closet, or WC, was the name given to the first flush toilets, devices used for washing away human waste. The water closet has a **cistern**, or tank full of water. When a handle or chain is pulled, water pours from the cistern, cleaning the toilet bowl. The cistern then fills automatically, ready for the next flush. The first water closets flushed into pits in the ground called **cesspits**. These were not always healthy as they could overflow. Waste was also piped into rivers and streams. When large networks of pipes, called sewers, were built under towns and cities in the mid-19th century, toilets were flushed into pipes that ran into them. The sewer system carried the waste away.

Gravity

Gravity is a force that pulls objects towards each other. The amount of pull depends on the **mass** of an object, or how much matter (solid, liquid or gas) there is in it. The gravity of the Earth pulls on the mass of other objects. This gives the objects **weight**. In space, where there are no objects to do the pulling, there is no weight. That's why astronauts can float in space.

Gravity is the force that makes things slide, fall or roll downwards. If you rest a ball on a slope, gravity will pull it so that it rolls down the slope, It also pulls you down when you jump into the air.

When a toilet is flushed, gravity pulls the water down and away. It also pulls down the ball in the cistern. This closes the exit tube as the cistern refills with water.

SUPER SEWERS

The first network of London sewers was built between 1856 and 1875, and was 133 km long. These sewers got rid of 454 million litres of sewage every day. Today, New York's sewage system deals with 6.3 billion litres every day.

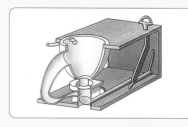

The pull of gravity from the Moon is less than from the Earth, so astronauts weigh less. They find it difficult to stand up because of the weak gravity.

Inventor's words

cesspit
cistern
gravity • mass
water closet
weight

Make a model lavatory

You will need

- plastic bottles and tray
- canes • cork mats
- double-sided tape
- play dough
- plastic tube
- cork • cardboard/box
- wire • bath plug • string

1 Cut a plastic bottle in half. Plug the spout with a cork mat and play dough to form a tight seal around the edges and central hole. Now make a hole in the lid. Push the plastic tube into a cork, and push the cork through the hole in the lid. Screw the lid on to the bottle.

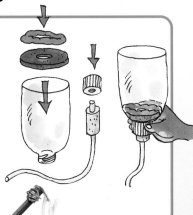

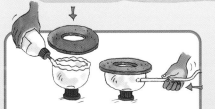

2 Cut the top off another bottle. Glue a cork mat toilet seat on top. Push the other end of the plastic tube into the back of the toilet bowl.

3 Cut a hole in a cardboard box. Push the toilet bowl into it. Slide a plastic tray underneath.

4 Glue a piece of cardboard behind the toilet. Cut a hole in it to support the bottle cistern. Fix in place. Glue a stick of cane to one side of the card partition and fix a wire hook to it. Now bind another cane to the stick with wire, making loops, as shown. Tie the bath plug on one side and the pull cord on the other.

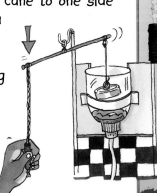

How can I print many books?

Making many copies of the same book is hard work and repetitive. Books have to be copied by hand or the letters stamped on a page with a wooden block - all very time-consuming. Johannes is sure there must be an easier way to copy books.

More and more people are learning to read. And they want books. But it takes a long time to produce them.

Johannes feels there must be a way of printing letters on a page using type, or letters carved into a block. But arranging the type and pressing the paper on to it still takes too much time.

I'm tired of working long hours. What can I use to press moveable type on to a page.

He tries to think of a way to speed up the process without simply using more workers. And the blocks of moveable type, type that can be shifted around, have to be easy to move.

WHAT CAN HE DO?

- He could hire a tribe of chimpanzees to do the work. Cheap - but might not be very accurate.

- He could use his metal-working skills to make special moulds for metal type. Good idea - but he still has to make a metal plate for each page.

- He could make the type small enough so that all the letters can be arranged again and again. But he'd still have to press it, and that takes time.

- He could fix his type to the bottom of a wine press. A good idea, but rather clumsy.

Why don't I build on the wine press idea with its screw mechanism? I'll build a frame so the printing block that holds the type can be firmly pressed against the paper on it. This way, I can print hundreds of pages a day.

The first book Gutenberg printed on his press was a Bible, in 1455. It had taken two years to complete.

Multiple copies

Printing means making copies of an original picture or text by transferring ink to paper or some other material. The Chinese were the first to print books. But in 1450, Johannes Gutenberg of Germany invented the first **printing press** using moveable type. The type was made into words and put under the press.

Ink was then spread on to the type and a piece of paper placed on top. The press was squeezed down on the paper with great force, created by a **screw** in the middle of the press. A long handle was attached to a pad under the screw to make a **lever**. As it was turned, the pad pressed down hard with the extra force created by the screw and lever.

Big screws

Most screws are used to fasten pieces of wood or other materials together. But sometimes big screws are used to create extra pushing power, or pressure, on objects.

A screw is a tube with a **ramp**, called a **thread**, that winds around it. When the screw is used to create pressure, it has a **nut** that moves up and down around the thread. It is the nut that moves rather than the screw. The nut has a handle to make it move.

When the nut is wound down, it moves much more slowly than if the tube was smooth, because it slides down the long ramp, or thread. If the handle is pushed, the nut, with a pad, or cutting device attached, slides down. A little sideways pressure on the handle creates a lot more downward pressure. The amount of pressure that is created depends on the length of both the handle and the thread.

A large screw can produce a big downwards force.

Inventor's words

auger • lever
nut • printing
printing press
ramp • screw
thread

Make a printing set

You will need

- cardboard
- white card • string
- glue • white paper
- paints and paintbrush

1 Cut large rectangles out of cardboard and white card. Glue the card to the cardboard backing.

2 Glue a piece of string in a pattern on each piece of card.

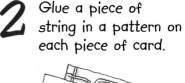

3 Cut small rectangles out of cardboard. Fold as shown, and stick down side tabs to make a 'grip'.

4 Carefully paint the string patterns in different colours.

5 Press the stamps on to plain paper to make prints.

How can I break down walls?

Mo has always enjoyed fireworks. But now he is interested in weaponry, especially spears and catapults. But they don't have the fire power he wants. He needs to invent a weapon that is powerful enough to knock down thick castle walls.

Mo designs a huge bow and arrow. But although it is big, it is too cumbersome to shoot his huge arrows at a wall.

Then he draws up plans for a mammoth catapult. But he can not think of a way to power it. A lever will create some power, but not enough for this machine.

Mo tries to think of other ways of shooting large objects at the enemy. He even thinks of wind-powered machines. But the power they make is never enough.

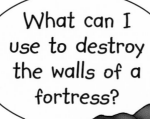

What can I use to destroy the walls of a fortress?

WHAT CAN HE DO?

- He could tie a huge boulder to a kite, fly it over the enemy and drop the boulder on the castle wall. But he'd need a kite as big as the castle!

- What about tying a rock to one of his rocket fireworks and shooting it at the castle? But the rockets are too small and too hard to aim.

- He could make a giant pea-shooter and fire the rockets through that. Now they'd be sure to hit the target.

- What if he put a lot of rockets in the tube with a big stone? The explosion would fire the rockets and the stone.

> I don't think I need the rockets, just the gunpowder that makes them fire. I'll make a bronze tube and stuff it with the powder. Then I'll drop in an iron ball. I'll make a small hole in the tube for a fuse, light it and – BANG! That should bring the walls down.

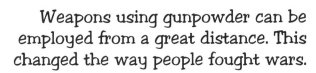

Weapons using gunpowder can be employed from a great distance. This changed the way people fought wars.

Big guns

A **cannon** is a large gun with a **calibre**, or diameter, of at least 2.5cm. Usually, it is fitted to a kind of carriage made of wood for easier transportation. Today, cannons are known as **artillery**, The first cannons may have been invented in China, but they were certainly used in Europe from about 1350. Most were made of wrought iron or bronze.

The first cannon balls were made of iron and weighed over 300kg. Later, they were made from stone, or stone covered with lead. The explosion from a cannon could hurl a ball over 1.5km. Castles were unable to withstand attacks by cannon fire. They declined as places of defence and instead became homes for the wealthy.

Gunpowder

When some substances burn, they change into something different. Petrol, for example, turns into a mixture of gases. Substances such as gunpowder burn very quickly. They turn into high-pressure gas. This means the gas expands, or gets bigger, very quickly. Substances that do this are called explosives.

Gunpowder is a type of explosive. If gunpowder is packed into a tube that is open at one end and set on fire, the expanding gas can shoot an object out of the tube at great speed. The first kind of gunpowder was called **black powder**. It was made of **saltpetre**, charcoal and sulphur. The ingredients were pressed together and broken into small pieces or used as a powder. Black powder was used to fire the first guns and cannons.

EXPLOSIVE TIMES

The use of gunpowder changed the way people lived in the Middle Ages. The old feudal system of lords and peasants relied on stone castles to protect the lords. But the castles could not stand up to pounding by heavy cannon balls, so the lords lost much of their power.

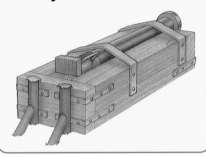

Gunpowder was invented in China. It was used in fireworks as well as cannons and pistols.

Inventor's words

artillery
black powder
calibre • cannon
expand
explosive
gunpowder
saltpetre

Make a cork-popping firearm

You will need

- large- and small-width cardboard tubes (make sure one fits inside the other with room to spare)
- cork coasters
- polystyrene sheet (about 10mm) and block (about 40mm)
- card • glue
- copper wire • string

1 Draw round the end of a large tube and cut out 2 cork discs, 3 thin polystyrene discs (plunger) and 1 thick polystyrene 'plug' for the bullet.

2 Push a thin tube through 3 thin polystyrene discs. Position the discs at equal distances along the tube, leaving 1/4 of the tube free at one end (the plunger handle).

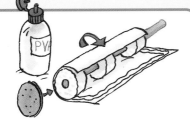

3 Wrap card around the discs, and glue. Glue a cork disc on to the front of the plunger and slide it into the large tube (barrel). It should fit tightly.

4 Fix wire hoops to the front of the polystyrene bullet and under the barrel. Join the bullet to the barrel by tying the ends of the string to the hoops. Glue a cork disc to the bullet.

Decorate, pop the bullet in the barrel – then prepare to attack!

How can I tell the time anywhere?

Peter is a locksmith. He has a problem when visiting customers' houses because he can't tell how long each job is taking. If he arrives late at his next job, his customers get angry. But his clock is too big and heavy to take with him. How else can he tell the time?

Peter is often asked to make new locks for people. This keeps him very busy. But sometimes he loses work because he is late arriving at the next job. When he is working, he doesn't think about the time. And when he does, it's often too late!

Peter must be able to tell the time wherever he is and at any time. But how can he if there isn't always a clock to hand?

> I need a time piece that I can carry around with me.

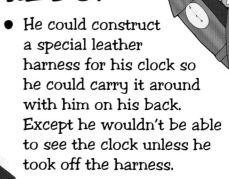

WHAT CAN HE DO?

- He could construct a special leather harness for his clock so he could carry it around with him on his back. Except he wouldn't be able to see the clock unless he took off the harness.

- Maybe he could make a cuckoo come out of the clock and 'cuckoo' every hour. Then at least he would hear the time on the hour.

- What if he made a clock small enough to hold in his hand? Just what he wants, but not possible with the weights needed to make it work.

- He needs to think of a way to make his clock work without using weights. Perhaps a spring could replace the weights, because Peter knows a spring has stored energy.

Because a coiled spring has energy stored in it, when I push the outside end of the spring, it bounces back. This kind of energy will work just like the energy in a big clock's weights. I think I'll use this energy to power my little clock.

The first watches, designed in the early 1500s, were worn around the neck or on a belt. Later, they were tied to a chain and put into a pocket.

Wristwatch

A **watch** is a device used for telling the time. Most watches are worn on the wrist. Some are powered by a clockwork motor that uses a spring, but many modern watches are powered by a tiny 'button' **battery**. A German locksmith called Peter Henlein was probably the first watchmaker. His watch only had an hour hand.

Henlein replaced the weight system of conventional clocks with a central spring called a **mainspring**. The mainspring enabled clockmakers to produce small, portable clocks that did not need to stand upright. Later, balance springs and escape lever mechanisms made watches more accurate and reliable.

Springs

A spring is a device such as a coiled piece of steel wire or a coiled flat steel bar. If it is pushed out of shape, a spring will return to its original form.

When a spring is out of shape, it has **potential energy** – energy that is stored up, ready to use later. When a spring is in this condition, it is said to be in **tension**. Tension is a pulling force that tries to stretch objects. When a spring is in tension, it is being stretched. When it is allowed to return to its original form, the tension is released and it no longer has potential energy. The tension in a spring is used to power machines such as watches. A tiny watch spring works with a lever to keep the watch hands turning around.

SPRING WEIGHT

A spring balance is a type of weighing machine. It contains a coil spring that is fixed to its top. The object to be weighed is hung on a hook at the lower end of the spring. A needle is pulled down along a scale, showing the weight of the object.

Small wheels regulate the movement of a watch and connect the spring to the hands on the dial.

Inventor's words

battery
mainspring
potential energy
spring
tension
watch

Make a fancy wristwatch

You will need

- toilet roll tube
- scissors
- coloured card
- glue • glitter
- sequins
- paper clips

1 Draw round the toilet roll tube. Cut out 2 thin rings from the end of the tube.

2 Cut out a pair of hands from white card and fix them to a decorated disc with a paper clip.

3 Cut out 4 discs of coloured card. Decorate 2 discs with glitter or sequins. Now stick the discs on either side of a card ring to make the watch face.

4 To make the wristband, cut a wide card ring from the toilet roll tube and cut this down the middle. Decorate.

5 Stick the wristband to the watch face. You can move the hands to tell the time.

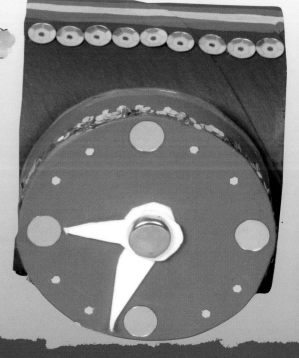

How can I see tiny objects clearly?

Anton is not happy about the cloth he buys. Too often it is not as good as he thinks it is. He wants to be sure he is buying only the best. But it is difficult to tell if the cloth is below standard because he can't always see the tiny flaws.

Anton buys and sells cloth all over Holland. Some merchants sell poor quality cloth, however, and Anton has been caught out.

He doesn't need to wear spectacles – his eyesight is perfect. But he does need to be able to see the cloth in more detail.

I must find a lens that can magnify at least 100 times.

He pulls the cloth fibres apart and looks at them under a magnifying glass. But that doesn't make the cloth look big enough. He needs something even better.

WHAT CAN HE DO?

- He could invent a potion that makes him shrink. He might become small enough to see the things he wants to see, then.

- Maybe he could buy only the most expensive cloth. But that would cost too much.

- He could make his own magnifying spectacle lenses. He might be able to magnify enough, but they would have to be very small to fit on his face.

- Better still, he could make just one lens. It wouldn't have to fit into spectacles frames at all.

I think one lens will work. I'll grind a tiny lens with a large magnification. I'll set the lens between two metal plates. Finally, I'll add an adjustable mount on which I can place my specimens.

The first microscopes could magnify an object 300 times.

Magnification

A **microscope** is an instrument used for studying tiny objects. The simplest microscope contains one or more **lenses**, pieces of glass with one or more sides cut in a curved shape. These produce an enlarged, or bigger, image of the object being looked at. Microscopes that use lenses are called light microscopes. They can **magnify** up to 4000 times the size of an object.

This allows scientists to look at things such as body cells, bacteria and pollen grains, which cannot be seen with the naked eye. An electron microscope uses a beam of tiny particles called **electrons** rather than light. An electron microscope can magnify over a million times the size of the object. Special electron microscopes are so powerful, they can show single **atoms**.

Reflection

Reflection is the way in which lightwaves or sound waves change direction when they hit something. When sound waves reflect off a wall, for example, we may hear an echo. When lightwaves reflect from a mirror, we see an image of the object.

Most light is reflected. What we see through our eyes are lightwaves reflected from the things around us. Without reflection we would not see any of the things around us. When there is no light, for example, on a dark night, we see nothing, even though the things we saw during the day are still there. Reflected light is what scientists see when they look through a microscope. They see the light waves reflected from the object they are looking at.

In daylight, we can see objects in detail. When it gets dark, we see only their outline.

ANIMALCULES

When Anton van Leeuwenhoek peered through his microscope, he discovered a world of tiny moving objects. He wrote about them to the scientists of the Royal Society in London and called them animalcules. We now know they were bacteria, protozoa and rotifers.

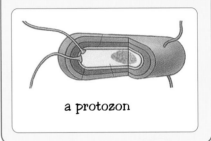

a protozon

Inventor's words

atom
electron • lens
magnify
microscope
reflection

Make a microscope

You will need

- cardboard tubes
- stickers
- wrapping paper
- glue • scissors
- plastic cake tray
- magnifying glass
- bottle cap • cardboard
- aluminium • foil
- thick wire

1 Decorate 2 cardboard tubes with wrapping paper and stickers. Cut one in half.

2 Glue the half-tubes to the base of the tall tube, so it stands upright.

3 Cut a deep notch into the top of the tall tube and slide in the handle of the magnifying glass. Glue a bottle cap on top.

4 Cut a hole halfway down the tall tube. Slot in a plastic cake tray, as shown.

5 Make a reflector by covering a cardboard disc with foil and attaching it to bent pieces of wire, as shown. Push the wire through the base of the microscope.

You can use your microscope to look at plants or dead flies, bees and butterflies.

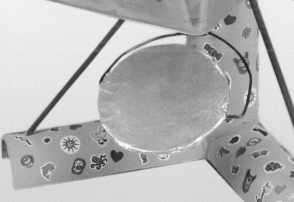

What is the temperature?

Gabriel knows when he feels too hot and when he feels too cold. Sometimes, though, he wants to know the exact temperature, so he needs to find a way measure it. But to do that, he will require some sort of instrument and a scale for measuring.

Gabriel wants to be able to record exact temperatures. But the devices used to tell temperatures are not accurate. If he wants to know the temperature of the air, he has to use either an air thermometer or an alcohol thermometer.

I must make an accurate thermometer and work out a scale of exact temperatures.

But these can only tell whether the temperature is going up or down. Gabriel wants numbers, although he isn't sure where they would start or end.

WHAT CAN HE DO?

- He could make his servant stand in the sun and shout out numbers as he gets hotter. But what if his servant has a cold.

- How about replacing the alcohol with milk in a tube? Oh dear, the milk just boils over.

- Better still, he could use the metal, mercury. It becomes bigger as it gets hotter - and it doesn't boil away.

- He could make a scale of numbers. But he needs a temperature that will always be the same for the top and bottom numbers.

I know that mercury expands when it is heated. I'll seal some in a thin tube. Then I'll mark the temperature that water, salt and ice freeze as zero. As the mercury rises in the tube, I'll mark off a scale up to 212°, which is when water boils.

On Fahrenheit's scale, the temperature at which pure water freezes is 32°.

Liquid metal

A **thermometer** is an instrument for measuring temperature. Most thermometers work on the scientific discovery that some substances **expand**, or get bigger, when they are heated. **Fahrenheit** invented the first accurate thermometer in 1724. Like most thermometers used by doctors today, his Fahrenheit's scale used the metal, **mercury**, as the measuring fluid.

The mercury is contained in a thin, glass tube. As the liquid mercury becomes warmer it expands, but the only direction in which it can go is up the tube. A scale on the side of the tube, or on the base to which it is fitted, indicates the temperature. Modern thermometers generally use the **Celsius** scale, where the temperature at which water freezes is marked as 0°.

Effect of heat

When something is heated, its atoms, the tiny building blocks that matter is made from, move around more quickly. And because they are moving more quickly, they move away from each other and take up more space. When something takes up more space, it expands.

When ice is heated up, its atoms begin to move more quickly and to move away from each other. Then, at a certain temperature, they are moving so quickly that the ice becomes a liquid, or water. This happens at 0° Celsius, or 0°C. At 100°C, the atoms of water are moving so quickly, they can't hold together and the water becomes a gas. The atoms in mercury move very quickly for a metal. While most metals are solid like ice, at normal temperatures, mercury is already a liquid. It only becomes a solid at a very cold -38.87°C.

LIQUID CRYSTAL THERMOMETER

A liquid crystal thermometer uses liquid crystals. The liquid crystals change colour as the temperature changes. This can be converted to a temperature scale. Liquid crystal thermometers are often used in aquariums to check water temperature.

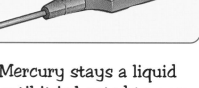

Mercury stays a liquid until it is heated to over 300 degrees Celsius. Then it becomes a gas.

Inventor's words

atom • Celsius
expand
Fahrenheit
matter • mercury
thermometer

Make your own thermometer

You will need

- shallow cardboard box
- 2 toilet rolls
- 2 kebab sticks
- thin white and red card
- paints and paintbrush
- PVA glue
- plastic bottle top

1 Draw, then cut a thermometer shape out of the bottom of the box. Paint it white.

2 Cut out 2 card discs the width of a toilet roll. Pierce a hole through each and glue one at the end of each toilet roll.

3 Make holes at both ends of the box. Push kebab sticks through these and then through the toilet rolls.

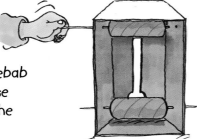

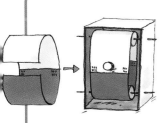

4 Staple the white and red card to make a strip. Feed this around the toilet rolls, and staple to fix in a roll. Glue on a bottle top 'button'.

5 Frame and paint the front of the box with weather pictures and symbols. Slide the button up and down to make the temperature rise and fall

How can I store electricity?

Coal and wood are wonderful sources of energy. But sometimes they are hard to find, and without them people will freeze. Alessandro imagines electricity would be a great source of energy. Think of all the energy in a flash of lightening. But how can he store electricity?

Alessandro hates to see people suffering because they have no fuel for heat or light. He knows about electricity and believes it can be used instead of coal and wood.

The ancient Greeks had made sparks by rubbing stones or metals together.

But a spark isn't enough. Alessandro wants electricity that flows constantly, just like a stream of water.

I want to build an electricity machine that I can turn on and off.

WHAT CAN HE DO?

- He could use a company of monks to rub their gowns against bits of amber to make static electricity. But it wouldn't be a constant flow.

- He could try to think of turning some other kind of energy into electrical energy - such as heat energy or chemical energy.

- Chemical energy seems best. He could study different substances to see if they might combine to make some form of electricity.

- What about investigating metals such as zinc and copper? Something seems to happen when they're dipped into salty water.

Why don't I take some disks of copper and zinc and pile them alternately on top of each other? Then I'll separate each one with a cardboard disk soaked in salt water. Together they'll produce a chemical change and then – hey presto! – I'll have all the electricity I want!

Count Volta displays his battery to the Emperor Napoleon in the early 19th century.

Creating a current

A **battery** is a device for turning chemical energy into electrical energy. Some batteries are disposable. This means that when one of the chemicals inside is used up, the battery is thrown away. Other batteries are **rechargeable**, which means they can be recharged with **electricity** and used again. A modern battery is generally made of layers of chemicals inside a metal can. These are much more efficient than Volta's battery. When a battery begins working, some of the chemicals inside break away and and eat at the metal container. The change to the can creates an electric current that flows out of the battery. Electricity is measured in volts, named after the inventor.

Electricity

Electricity is a type of energy. It can be used to create light in a lightbulb or heat in an electric fire. It can also be used to power trains or cars. And it comes from part of an atom.

All **matter** is made up of tiny particles, or bits, called atoms. Each atom has a nucleus at its centre and one or more **electrons** spinning around the **nucleus**. In some kinds of matter, the electrons can be pushed from one atom to another. And as these electrons move, they push other electrons along as well. This makes a stream of electrons. Each electron has a small amount of energy and only moves a short distance when it is pushed.

ELECTRIC LIGHT

When electricity reaches a lightbulb, it has to pass through a thin thread of wire called a filament. The filament is so thin, the electrons cannot move easily through it. As they have to push so hard, the electrons make the atoms in the filament move faster. This makes the filament heat up and glow.

But inside a wire or battery there are millions and millions of electrons. So when you turn on a switch, you start a big stream of electrons moving.

The acid in a lemon works like the chemicals in a battery, to activate this digital clock.

Inventor's words

atom • battery
electricity
electron
filament • matter
nucleus
rechargeable

Dragon with flashing eyes

You will need

- chicken wire
- newspaper strips soaked in half-water half-PVA solution
- 2 torch bulbs
- 4 long pieces of copper wire
- tape
- 4 AA batteries
- paints and brush

1 Mould the chicken wire into a dragon-shape. Cover it with glue-soaked paper strips. Dry and repeat.

2 Tape one copper wire to the end of a bulb, and another to the side of it. Wrap one wire in tape to insulate. Now tape both wires together.

3 Cut an eyehole in the dragon's head. Pass the wire through the hole and out of another made in the back of the head. Push the bulb into the socket.

4 Tape two AA batteries together. Tape up the end of each wire to either end of the battery set. Push the top wire down on to the battery end to make the eye light up. Repeat for the other eye.

5 Stick on card wings, then paint and decorate your dragon.

WARNING

Test the eye bulbs are still connected and working at every stage of construction. Leave the top wire disconnected when not in use.

Glossary and index

Air resistance Pressure of air against an object as it moves. Air resistance causes friction, which slows an object down. p.10

Artillery Group of large, heavy guns used in war. It is also the branch of an army that uses these weapons. p.25

Atom Tiny part of an element, or simple substance, made up of one or more electrons that move around a nucleus. The nucleus is made up of neutrons and protons. All the atoms in an element are the same. p.33, 38, 42

Auger Large screw used to drill holes in the ground. p.22

Battery Device that supplies an electric current by turning chemical energy into electrical energy. It contains two kinds of electric conductor joined together by a chemical paste. p.29, 41, 42

Bifocal Type of lens with two focal points, used in spectacles. One allows the eye to see close up; the other allows it to see far away. p.14

Black powder Explosive material made of saltpetre, charcoal and sulphur. p.26

Calibre Inside diameter of a gun barrel, or the diameter of a bullet. p.25

Cannon Large gun with a calibre of more than 2.5cm. Cannons are usually placed on a carriage so they can be moved about easily. p.25

Canopy Expanding, or opening part, of a parachute or a hanging cover, forming a shelter. p.9

Catapult Machine used in warfare to throw boulders or other large weights. There are torque and lever type catapults. p.4, 5, 6

Celsius Unit used to measure temperature, where water freezes at 0° C and boils at 100° C. Named after its inventor, the Swedish astronomer Anders Celsius. p37, 38

Cesspit Pit dug in the ground to take sewage from houses. p.17

Cistern Storage tank used to contain water for flush toilets. p.17, 18

Concave Shape that bends inwards to make a hollow. Used in lenses to bend light outwards. p.13, 14

Convex Shape that bends outwards to make a mound. Used in lenses to bend light inwards. p.13, 14

Electricity Type of energy used as an electric current to power machines. p.40, 41, 42

Electron Tiny speck of matter that is usually part of an atom. An electron moves in an orbit around the nucleus of an atom. p.33, 42

Envelope Canopy, or expanding part of a parachute. p.9

Expand Become bigger or take up more space. Most gases, liquids and solids expand when they are heated. p.26

Explosive Substance that expands suddenly, making a loud noise and giving off a huge amount of energy. p.26

Fahrenheit Unit used to measure temperature, where water freezes at 32° F and boils at 212° F. Named after its inventor, the German physicist Gabriel Dante Fahrenheit. p.37

Filament Thin wire, usually made of tungsten, that is found inside an electric light bulb. When an electric current is passed through it, the filament glows, giving the bulb its light. p.42

Gravity Force that pulls objects towards each other. Gravity causes objects to have weight. p.18

Gunpowder Substance made of potassium nitrate, charcoal and sulphur that explodes when it is lit, or ignited. It is the earliest known propellant. p.26

Lens Piece of glass or plastic that has been ground so that both sides curve either inwards or outwards. Lenses are used to bend light. p.12, 13, 14, 32, 33

Lever Bar or rod that moves around a fulcrum. The effort of pressing down on one end lifts a load. One of the six simple machines used to do work. p.6, 21

Magnify Make an object look larger. A lens is used to magnify objects. p.33

Mainspring The principal, or main, spring in a watch or clock. p.29

Mass Amount of matter in an object, measured in kilograms. All objects have mass and take up space. p.18

Matter Everything in the universe that occupies space and has weight. Matter can be a solid, liquid or gas. p.38, 42

Mercury An element. It is a silvery metal that is liquid at room temperature. Mercury is used in thermometers. p.36, 37, 38

Missile Object fired from a weapon that is aimed at a particular target. p.5, 6

Nucleus Centre of an atom containing protons and neutrons. p.42

Nut Flat piece of metal with four or six sides and a hole in the middle. The hole has a spiral groove called a thread that fits with the thread on a bolt. p.22

Optician Person who makes or sells spectacles, and who is also trained to correct defects in people's eyes. p.14

Parachute Device for lowering people or things slowly through the air. Cords lead from an envelope, or canopy, to a harness. The envelope uses air resistance to slow down the descent of the person using the parachute. p.9, 10

Potential energy Stored energy. Electrical energy in a battery is stored energy, or energy waiting to be used. p.30

Printing Process of producing copies of an original picture or text by transferring ink to paper or other material. p.21

Printing press Machine for printing that uses a press to squeeze ink on to paper. Early presses used screw mechanisms. Modern ones use rollers. p.21

Ramp Inclined plane, or sloping surface. p.22

Rechargeable Battery that can have its components recharged and used again. p.41

Reflection An identical image seen in a mirror or other reflecting material, so that the left side of the image is the reflection of the right side of the object. p.34

Refraction The process of bending or changing direction. Lightwaves can be refracted, or bent, by passing through a transparent object such as a lens or prism. p.14

Retina Layer of special cells that line the back of the eyeball. Light focuses on the retina through the lens and is turned by the retina into signals that are sent to the brain. p14

Ripcord Cord that releases the canopy of a parachute after the parachutist has leaped into the air. p.9

Saltpetre Substance whose chemical name is potassium nitrate, used to make gunpowder. p.26

Screw Type of simple machine with an inclined plane wrapped in a spiral around a thin rod. It is used as a fastener or to create pressure in pressing machines. p.21, 22

Spectacles Frames that contain lenses. The lenses allow the wearer to see things more clearly. p.13, 14

Spring Coiled piece of steel wire or bands of steel fixed together. Springs return to their original shape after being forced out of shape. When out of shape, a spring has potential energy. p.29, 30

Streamline An object that cuts through air or water easily is called streamlined, or aerodynamic. p.10

Suspension lines Strong cords that connect a parachutist's harness to the parachute. p.9

Tension Type of force. It is a pull that tries to stretch an object. p.30

Thermometer Instrument for measuring temperature. Most contain liquids that expand when they are heated. The liquid's position in a tube registers the temperature. p.36, 37, 38

Thread Inclined plane that spirals down the side of a screw. p.22

Torque Effort needed to twist a shaft. p.6

Trebuchet Large catapult that uses a sling action to throw objects. p.5

Watch Small time-keeping device that works in the same way as a clock. p.29, 30

Water closet Device for flushing away human waste that uses a cistern full of water and a lever. The lever releases the water into the pan. The water is then flushed away into a sewer system and fresh water takes its place. p.17

Weight Amount gravity pulls on an object, measured in kilograms. p.18

Tools and Materials

Almost all of the materials in this book can be found around the house or bought at your local art or craft shop. If you cannot find the exact item, try and replace it with something similar.

Most of the models will stick fast with PVA glue or even wallpaper paste. However, some materials need a stronger glue – so take care when using these as they may damage your clothes and even your skin. Ask an adult to help you.

Always protect furniture with newspaper or a large cloth, and cover your clothes by wearing an apron.

User Care

Take special care when handling sharp tools such as scissors, pointed gadgets, pieces of wire or craft knives. Ask an adult to help you when you need to use them.